GREAT
ANSWERS
to DIFFICULT
QUESTIONS
about DEATH

other books in the series

Great Answers to Difficult Questions about Sex
What Children Need to Know
Linda Goldman
ISBN 978 1 849 05804 9

Great Answers to Difficult Questions about Divorce
What Children Need to Know
Fanny Cohen Herlem
ISBN 978 1 84310 672 2

Great Answers to Difficult Questions about Adoption
What Children Need to Know
Fanny Cohen Herlem
ISBN 978 1 84310 671 5

of related interest

Grief in Children
A Handbook for Adults
Second Edition
Atle Dyregrov
Foreword by Professor William Yule
ISBN 978 1 84310 612 8

by the same author

Children Also Grieve
Talking about Death and Healing
Linda Goldman
ISBN 978 1 84310 808 5

GREAT ANSWERS to DIFFICULT QUESTIONS about DEATH

What Children Need to Know

Linda Goldman

Jessica Kingsley Publishers
London and Philadelphia

First published in 2009
by Jessica Kingsley Publishers
116 Pentonville Road
London N1 9JB, UK
and
400 Market Street, Suite 400
Philadelphia, PA 19106, USA

www.jkp.com

Library of Congress Cataloging in Publication Data
A CIP catalog record for this book is available from the Library of Congress

British Library Cataloguing in Publication Data
A CIP catalogue record for this book is available from the British Library

ISBN 978 1 849 05805 6

Printed and bound in the United States by
Thomson-Shore Inc., 7300 W. Joy Road, Dexter, MI 48130

Contents

Preface

Children's questions are a window to their soul –
and a mirror to their inner thoughts and feelings

Death is a difficult and sensitive topic to discuss with children. So often adults feel at a loss for words. Without knowing what to say or how to say it, many parents and professionals avoid children's questions. Some refuse to respond at all. Eight-year-old Alice explained a disturbing event. She told her teacher about her dad's death during the very first week of school. Her teacher never said a word. Infuriated and saddened, Alice asked over and over, "Why didn't my teacher ever say anything back?"

Often girls and boys share how angry and alone they feel at being dismissed or ignored when asking questions about the death of a loved one. "Where did my mom go?", "Why did Dad have to die?", "Did my doggy suffer?", "Will I die too?" are very common thoughts for girls and boys to have.

Responding with care can normalize children's uncomfortable ideas and feelings. Acknowledging their questions is a valuable way of reassuring them and helping them to feel safe.

Honoring children's questions

We may feel terrified when confronted by a child with a question about death, and send a conscious or unconscious message inhibiting further discussion. When adults respond to questions in ways that are more complicated than necessary, children can become overwhelmed. When adults limit replies or refuse to answer, children get the message. Death is a closed topic – don't ask again.

Joey's mom wanted to know, "What do I do when my 5-year-old asks so many questions about death?" One health care professional responded to Joey's mother in this way:

"My daughter Annie is 5. She also asked too many questions about death. I explained to her she could only ask two questions a day. If she asked more than that she would need to go to her room for a half hour and think about it. This really worked. Within one month's time Annie never asked another question about death."

Annie got the message in no uncertain terms – stop asking about death.

Placing restrictions or discounting children's questions will tend to stop children asking them. Our goal is to create an environment where all questions are welcomed, accepted, and responded to openly and without judgment. The purpose of this book is to share simple and direct dialogues about death to facilitate open communication. Such comfortable language is a way caring adults can share appropriate responses that satisfy and nurture young people.

Developmental understandings

Children re-grieve at different developmental stages. During early childhood they are usually satisfied with a simple definition and explanation. They see death as reversible and have egocentric ideas involving magical thinking. Many times they believe they caused their person's death.

As they get older they become more curious about the facts of the death, and may come back to it at ages 8, 9, and 10 and revisit the death with new interest and inquisitiveness. In pre-adolescence and adolescence they have a strong need to look to their own age group to find answers.

At this age girls and boys begin to see that death is not reversible. Life is finite. Young people begin to form their own spiritual belief system and look to their peers for support and understanding. They feel empowered to become advocates for causes related to their person's death.

What to say and how to say it

Sammy, age 6, asked his mom, "Why did Dad have to die?" Mom responded, "Why do *you* think?" Instead of answering for him, Sammy's mother created a non-judgmental space to hear her son's thoughts and feelings. "I think Dad died because I was a bad boy and God was mad at me." Sammy shared his age-appropriate magical thinking that he was the cause of his father's death. By expressing this fear out loud, Mom was able to talk about

Dad's death and the facts surrounding it: "Dad died from having heart disease. His heart had been sick for many years and the doctors had been helping him for a long time. It was not your fault."

Children's questions about death reveal the essence of their inner world and create a deep insight into their grief process. They often reflect fears and worries that are easier for them to ask about than to dialogue directly. Listening with an *inner ear* to the feelings behind their questions is a valuable tool for exposing unsaid thoughts and feelings and helping boys and girls release them in a safe way.

The following chapters include suggestions of useful language on the topic of death. Each chapter contains practical, age-appropriate dialogue which respects and honors children's questions on this subject. These dialogues encourage an open forum for discussion. Caring adults can discuss death with kids in ways that ease anxiety and build confidence for further exploration of ideas.

Children's questions are the key that unlocks the door to understanding their grief so that we can help them.

CHAPTER 1

Why did my mom have to die?

Telling a child that a parent or sibling has died is quite difficult for all of us. Giving a reason for this death is even harder. We often worry about the explanation and are challenged to find just the right words. We wonder if children are too young to talk to about this subject. Can they handle it?

Working with children and issues of death has deepened my certainty they can handle this sensitive conversation. What *is* difficult for our children is to feel excluded, left out, or lied to. Many boys and girls feel comforted with concise and truthful answers, especially at young ages. If explanations are too long with too much information, some children may just tune out of the conversation. When children get a little older they want to know more about the facts about what happened to their person and then look for peer support.

A good beginning for young children is to give a simple and straightforward response. Be open to inviting other questions that may follow. As they get older, they may revisit a loved one's death wanting more details and deeper understanding. As children grow up they continue to ponder the question of why their person had to die.

The following case study shares 6-year-old Tanya's experience after her mother's death. It traces Tanya's questions at ages 6, 9, and 11. Children re-grieve at different developmental stages, and Tanya's grief reactions change as she matures, displaying evolving age-appropriate thoughts and feelings.

Tanya (6): a case study

Tanya was 6 years old when her life changed forever. She was referred to me for grief therapy after her mother died. In our first session Tanya shared an important memory. She explained she had run home from school, opened the door to say hi to her mom – and realized her house was filled with people, talking and crying. Her dad was sitting in the corner, his head in his hands, rocking back and forth. "What did you think was going on?" I wondered. She shook her head and looked down. "I didn't know."

Tanya continued to describe the scenario. Uncle Matt had appeared, put his arm around her and whispered, "I have some bad news for you. Your mom has died". Then she began to cry in my office. "You seem so sad, Tanya. Can you tell me why?" I asked. "Uncle Matt told me my mom died," she shared. "I had heard the words but they didn't seem real. I couldn't even see through all of my tears. How could my mom have died? We just had breakfast together that morning. I still can't believe she won't be back." She again burst into tears.

"It is hard to believe that someone you love could die. It's so sad to imagine them not being here," I explained. "Do you remember what was going through your mind?" Tanya looked up at me with her big brown eyes and said, "I do remember. The words kept racing over and over in my mind. My mom is dead. This isn't real. This isn't happening to me. Then a big question came to me that wouldn't leave. Why did my mom have to die?"

Why did my mom die?

You have asked an important question and deserve the answer. Your mom died because she was walking across the street and a car ran into her. The car hit her so hard she was badly injured. It made her body stopped working.

If you think of any more questions let me know.

Is my mom coming back?

No, death is not reversible. It can't change back into life. It's not like magic. Mom is not coming back. Lots of children your age think death is reversible. They feel their person is coming back even though they have been to the funeral, the burial, and picture them in heaven.

I wrote my mom a letter and put it in the mailbox. Why doesn't she write back?

She can't write back. She is dead. Her body has stopped working. Sadly, death isn't reversible and Mom can't write back.

Today's my mom's birthday. Why didn't anybody mention her name? That makes me angry.

I can understand why you are angry. It is such an important day and it seems like you are thinking about Mom a lot and don't have anyone to talk to about her. Some people are afraid to bring her up with you. They think they are making you sad by remembering. Others worry about the right words to use. They don't understand it's your mom's birthday and you are already thinking about her and want to share your thoughts.

My mom had a cold. I didn't make her stay home that day. Is it my fault she died?
Definitely not. You did not cause her death and you are in no way responsible. Girls and boys your age often have these kinds of guilty thoughts. They think if their person died, it must be their fault. That is not true and not what happened. A car hit your mom and that is the real reason she died.

Tanya (9)

It's been three years since my mom died. Why am I still wondering about why she died?
That's a good question. Lots of children re-grieve when they get older and think about their person's death in different ways. At your age children usually want to know more details about their person's death.

I want to know more of the facts about why my mom had to die. Can you tell me how to find out the details?
I will tell you whatever I know. Why don't you make a list of the things you want to find out the most? Most children your age are curious about the facts. They think of questions they couldn't have thought about when they were younger.

What happened at the accident? Who was the person driving the car? Where did it happen?

These are important questions, Tanya. If I don't know all of the answers we can find out together. The accident happened at the end of your street, the corner of Elm and Mulberry. A man named Mr. Adams didn't see your mom crossing the street and struck her down with his car. The doctors said your mom's heart stopped and she died right away. By the time the ambulance came she had stopped breathing.

But what happened to Mom's body?

I don't know that answer. Maybe your dad does. Why don't you ask him?

Tanya (11)

It's been so long since Mom died. I still get sad. Why do I miss her so much?

Lots of children miss their mom for a long, long time. Sometimes birthdays and holidays make them remember. Sometimes seeing a butterfly reminds them of their person and brings back a special time.

No one can take your mom's place. I know you told me you miss her at school plays and piano recitals. You realize she isn't there and feel sad. Maybe you could wear her heart necklace for good luck and invite your favorite Aunt Nancy to be there for you.

What can I do? I still don't understand why she had to die. Can you help me understand why she died?

You are 11 and growing up. Young people at your age are looking for different answers. It's understandable you want to know even more about your mom's death. Maybe you can ask your relatives and your mom's friends if they can explain the reasons for her death. You might get lots of surprising answers.

Can you tell me about the man who was driving the car? Someone told me he was a drunk driver.

I'm glad you found out the answer to your question. He was a drunk driver. That should help you make more sense of the car crash. It wasn't your fault or your mom's. It was the man who drove the car. He had been drinking too much alcohol and wasn't driving carefully. He had a very bad driving record and had been arrested several times.

I'm never going to drink and drive. And I won't let my friends. I am so angry. He should be punished. Why wasn't he paying attention? What was he doing? Did he go to jail?

I agree, Tanya. Drunk driving should be punished. And you have every right to feel angry. Let's talk to your father and find out what happened. It's helpful to ask family members about different things. I am glad your dad explained the drunk driver was arrested and tried for drunk driving, and found guilty. He did spend some time in prison. We could also look up newspaper articles about your mom's death in the library and find out more facts about what happened and the statistics of drunk driving accidents and deaths.

No matter how much time he spent in prison it wouldn't be enough – not enough to bring back my mom. Can I help stop drunk drivers?
Yes, you can. You could write a story or give a talk. Do you have any other ideas?

I thought of a project. I would like to help my school have an assembly on drunk driving. Do you think I could tell my story to other children?
Yes I do. That's a great idea. It might help a lot of children. Because a drunk driver killed your mom, becoming an advocate against drinking and driving can help give meaning to your mom's death. Service to others adds significance to why your mom died. And you can help other kids to think more about the consequences of drinking and driving. It just may save lives.

Who can I talk to about this? Who would understand?
Sometimes other children your age that have been through similar things can understand. Young people your age like to talk to other children for support. Maybe a peer support grief group could be helpful. Why don't we find a grief support group for children your age? You could try it one time and see if you like it.

Concluding thought

Children are unique and so are their questions. We must respond to *every child* according to his or her age and developmental understanding. We must also respond to the *same child* in different ways as they get older and revisit the death of a loved one at a new age and new level of understanding. We also need to recognize that not every question has a factual answer. Some things can be mysteries.

CHAPTER 2

What does dead mean? How do people die?

Children need to be told the truth about a death in an age-appropriate way. They usually know when they are being lied to. So often lies create a secondary loss of trust of their emotional environment.

There are many ways people die. Often adults have difficulty in finding the precise words to use to explain a fatal illness, sudden accident, murder, suicide, or natural or man-made catastrophe. They are surprised when many girls and boys are satisfied with simple and honest responses appropriate to their developmental stage. Six-year-old Rebecca asked, "How did Mommy die?" "She got very ill," might be just enough of a response.

Greg (5): a case study

Five-year-old Greg was sad. His pet gerbil, Jasper, had died. Jasper was lying in the cage very still. Greg started screaming and crying and Mom ran into the room to see what happened. "Something is wrong with Jasper. He isn't moving. I'm scared." Mom had a tear in her eye.

"Jasper died, sweetie." Greg put his hands over his ears. "No! No! That can't be true."

What does death mean?
Death means when the body stops working. Sometimes people die when they are very, very, very old, or very, very, very ill, or they are so, so, so injured that the doctors and nurses can't make their bodies work anymore. Jasper is dead. It is sad. He will not move, not be warm, and not be alive again.

What can't you do when your body doesn't work?
You can't eat, you can't play, you can't watch TV – you can't even breathe. Jasper has died. His body is getting cold. It stopped working and he can't even run in his cage.

But where does his body go?
Animals and people can be buried in the ground. When you are ready, we can find a box to bury Jasper in. We can put a soft blanket inside with Jasper's body and you can put in something special too.

Can I put in a picture of me? He would like that. Then he won't feel so alone. Let's put his toy in too.
That sounds like a great idea. We can decorate the box with things that remind you of Jasper.

Can we bury Jasper together?

Yes, it is nice to have a ceremony where everyone can do something. You could say a prayer, light a candle, send off a balloon, or plant a flower. It feels good to do something special after a death.

Alex (9)

My mom died of cancer. What does cancer mean?

Cancer is an illness that comes from very, very, tiny round parts in your body called cells. The cells are so small we can't see them without a microscope. Most cells are healthy and help your body live. Cancer cells are different. They don't look or grow like normal cells. Sometimes they grow so fast they crowd the good cells out, and they crowd together. This is called a tumor.

How did it make my mom die?
Your mom had a cancer tumor. All of the cancer cells kept growing and growing until the normal cells couldn't work anymore. The tumor got so big it made your mom's body stop working.

Why do all the good people like my mom die young?
That's a difficult question to answer. Your mom was too young to die. Children and adults wonder why such a good person like your mom got cancer. Sometimes we just don't know all the answers.

Kyle (11; brother killed in drive-by shooting)

My mom said my brother Tony died in an accident. A boy at school said he was murdered. How did Tony really die?
Tony was murdered. Another name for being murdered is killed. Killed is when someone chooses to make someone else's body stop working. A stranger killed Tony with a gun. This stranger was riding in a car and shot him when he was walking down the street.

Did they find the person that shot him?
The police are working very hard to find this person. You might hear more information from children at school, TV, or even the Internet. It is important you check out what you know with me or your parents, so that you

know the facts about what happened and not believe rumors from friends, relatives, or the media.

I don't like to talk about the shooting. That worries my mom. Is it OK?

Sometimes it takes a while for children to react to a traumatic death. You might need time before you talk about it. Your parents may worry about you not showing a lot of emotion – like anger or sadness or even fear. You can explain to them you are just not ready to share your feelings with them and that when you are ready you will let them know. It is OK to ask for some time and space.

I keep imagining what happened. It's scary. Can I get shot?

Sometimes people die in very scary ways. It is hard when you keep imagining the killing and think that it could happen to you. If you make a drawing about how you think Tony died, it might help remove those difficult pictures in your mind by putting them on paper. Then you might be less afraid.

Thinking about your own safety is important. The police are working very hard to find the killer. You can help yourself feel safe by locking the doors to your house, knowing emergency numbers like 911 (USA) and 999 (UK), and walking with a friend or adult and not alone.

Tommy (8; dad died of suicide)

How did my dad die?

Tommy, it sounds like you're not sure how your dad died. Can you tell me what you think happened?

People say heart attack, stroke, drugs, or they just don't know. What really happened?

Your dad died of suicide. Suicide is when someone chooses to make his or her own body stop working. Your dad had been very, very sad for a long time. That is called depressed. He would sleep all day, or be angry and not know why, forget things, and get overwhelmed with his sad feelings. One day he took too many pills and it made his body stop working. He left Mom a note saying he didn't want to live anymore. Mom said he loved you a lot and he was proud of what a great football player you are.

Mary (12; dad died of suicide)

I can't even remember my dad. He died when I was 2. My mom says it was an accident. I didn't believe her anymore. I'd heard so many stories I decided to look up the facts in the newspaper. It was suicide. How can I ever believe my mom again?

It is understandable you have lost trust in your emotional world. Your mom has hidden the truth from you for a long time. She was afraid you wouldn't understand about suicide and she couldn't find the words to explain it to a young child. Avoiding your questions as you grew up only made the lie bigger. Now you know the facts. He jumped off a bridge and witnesses watched it happen. He was very depressed because he had been out of work for a long time.

I feel better knowing the truth. Now everything makes sense. Is it wrong to be so angry with my mom?
No, it makes a lot of sense. It is so difficult to discover someone you love has been lying to you, even if they had the best of intentions. It makes you wonder if you can ever trust them again. Some children feel it is more painful to be lied to during childhood than to learn the truth about the way their parent died, even if the truth is hard to handle. Maybe you can talk to Mom about your anger.

Concluding thought

Telling children the truth in age-appropriate ways is helpful in securing their trust. In order to communicate we need clear and simple language for dialogues. Sometimes children hear different stories about what happened to their person from friends, relatives, or even the news. They want to find out the real answer. Preparing answers and dialogues using definitions of death and of specific ways people die can encourage open communication and maintain a level of honesty for the grieving child.

CHAPTER 3

Where was God when I needed him? How could God let my brother die?

Children and grown-ups often have questions about God after someone dies. The one question they ask most often is "How could God let this happen?" It is common after a death to be angry with God and feel abandoned. Some children lose faith and wonder how a loving God could do such an awful thing. Adults wonder why terrible things happen to nice people too. It helps to know that people have a wide range of feelings toward God like anger, frustration, and disappointment and that it is OK to share these feelings. In fact – expressing these feelings can help to let go of them.

Sara (5): a case study

Clichés often block a young child's understanding of death because they take language literally. Many of these clichés relate to God. Five-year-old Sara was told it was *God's will* that her grandma died – that God took

Grandma to be with Him. He loved her so much because she was so good. She misinterpreted the explanation thinking if God could take Grandma, God could take her too. This idea about God created unnecessary anxiety.

My mom said Grandma was so good God took her away. Aren't I good too? Why doesn't God want me?

You are good, Sara, and so was your grandma. God doesn't take people away just because they are good. They die. No one knows why some people live a short life or why some live a longer life. No one knows the time they will die. Everyone dies. That is a part of life, whether they do good or bad things.

Julian (7)

My brother Sam was so ill. We took him to the doctor's and gave him all of his medicine. How could God still have let him die?

Julian, sometimes there are no answers. I know you and your mom and dad did everything you could to take care of Sam and help him be healthy. It's hard not to blame God when everyone tried so hard. Lots of people feel let down by God when someone they loved dies and they have tried so hard to keep them alive. Other people believe God doesn't let people live or die, but that God stays with you and helps you when you are going through something hard. What do you think?

I think Sam is in heaven with God and they are watching over me. Do you think God is helping Sam in heaven?
That's a good question. It might help you to feel better if you think God is taking care of Sam. Maybe you can imagine God giving Sam medicine and keeping him healthy in heaven. Drawing a picture of God with Sam, saying a prayer, or lighting a candle feels good too.

Grown-ups can't always give you all the answers about God and death and what happened after Sam died. Sometimes life and death can be mysteries, and there might be a bigger picture than you and I can possibly imagine.

Adam (11)

I am so angry with God. I hate God. It's God's fault my dad got hit by a car.
Anger, blame, hatred, and love are feelings lots of children have towards God after a death. You need to know that's normal and OK. Sometimes I get angry with God too. Sometimes I wonder where he was when someone I loved died. Sometimes I am grateful for his help in getting through my grief. Sometimes I wish I had more answers to my own questions too. There are just some things no one knows.

I can't even say a prayer. I don't believe in God anymore!
I understand you are so angry with God that you feel you can't believe in him anymore. Sometimes we are so upset

after someone dies we need someone or something to blame – and that can be God. You might feel like that for a while and that is OK. In a few weeks or months you might change your mind. You might see it wasn't anyone's fault – it was just a bad accident that happened that no one could change. You might need some time.

The only question I have now is why did God have to kill my dad?
Right now you feel deeply disappointed in God for not saving your dad's life. I can't answer your question for you, but can I talk to you about how you feel about God? How do you feel about what happened to your dad? What are your thoughts and beliefs about God? That might help you to understand your feelings a little better.

Amelia (9)

After my sister died I wanted to know more about God. What is God? What do different people believe?
It seems like you are doing a lot of thinking about God. God can be a special force, nature, a spiritual being, or love itself. How anybody feels about God or sees God is very personal. There is no good or bad way. Some people believe they have a personal relationship with God. Others feel religion brings them closer to God. And still others don't even believe in God.

Some people believe that when you die your soul or the part of you that is God goes to God. Others believe you come back in another form – a plant, an animal, or another human being. Still others believe you are buried in the ground and it helps the plants and animals to grow.

Concluding thought

It is crucial to respect a child's belief system. "What do you believe happens after someone dies?" is a good open-ended question that opens a dialogue for exploration. Adults can engage children in discovering their own spiritual understandings rather than telling them what they should believe. Then the dialogue can be expanded to an acceptance that many people have different belief systems. It's OK to admit that no one has all the answers about God and the meaning of life and death.

CHAPTER 4

Where is my person? What is heaven?

Children tend to have an ongoing and ever-present relationship with their person that died. They like to find the place where they feel they can make a connection with a loved one. Some children think their mom or dad is in the breeze that goes by, a butterfly in the sky, or that they really visit them in a dream or vision. Others find comfort and meaning in napping on Mom's bed, visiting the cemetery, going to the street where Dad died, or sitting in Grandpa's favorite chair. Visiting these places can be reassuring and important in maintaining their connection with their special person.

Research suggests that a majority of children place their person that died in a place called *heaven*. They may also think their person is in the ground, is coming back home, or is living with God and the angels at the same time. When children ask questions about heaven, it is a good clue that they are thinking about it. Asking them to explain how they see heaven allows them to share their images and beliefs.

Heaven is the most popular place in which kids and adults place their friends, relatives, and pets after they die. Even pop culture has songs about "seeing you in heaven," "heaven is in your eyes" and "heavenly angels." Most religions talk about a place called heaven where people live with God and this imagery can be very comforting.

Marc (12): a case study

Marc was 12 when his dad got killed in a plane crash. They played sports together all of the time. Dad was the coach of his basketball team. After his dad's death Marc played many of his games thinking of his dad. He was so happy when he won the award for the best athlete in his school – a big gold trophy with his name engraved on it. But he missed his dad being at the ceremony to see him receive it.

"Where do you think Dad is?" he asked his mother. Mom replied, "I'm not sure. Sometimes I feel he is with me when I hear a bird chirp. Dad loved birds. Sometimes I talk with him at the cemetery." Marc decided to visit the cemetery the next day, and took his trophy to show him. Sitting by Dad's gravestone, he told him all about the sports ceremony: "It was great, but I missed you."

Then he sat quietly for a long time. When he got home Marc told his mom he finally felt at peace – as if Dad was really with him for the first time since he died. Yet he wondered if that was a strange way to feel.

Is it OK to feel like my dad is really at the cemetery?
Yes, it is OK. The cemetery looks like a meaningful place for you. It's a spot you have found where you feel you can be with your father in some way. Some children go to the cemetery, sit in Grandpa's favorite chair, or some even nap on Mom's bed. Others create conversations like you did or leave special pictures and flowers. You seemed so happy to sit by Dad's gravestone and share your sports ceremony and trophy with him. That's nice.

Even though the cemetery feels peaceful, I still can't believe my dad is dead. I didn't say goodbye. Can I go to the spot where Dad was killed?

I really understand why you want to go to the location where the plane crash happened. These places can have personal and important meaning. Let your mom or I know when you feel ready to take this trip. It can be upsetting when you don't get the chance to say goodbye, especially when a sudden death occurs away from home. Bringing something for your dad, retracing the details of the incident, and just being at the site where Dad died creates a unique moment to feel his presence and say goodbye. Maybe the visit would make his death feel more real for you. You could even write Dad a goodbye letter.

Sally (6)

My aunt Jenny told me Mom had gone on a long trip. Why didn't she take me with her? And how could she go on a long trip if she died of cancer?

Sally, I know your aunt Jenny told you that your mom went on a long trip and Dad had explained Mom died from a disease called cancer. Aunt Jenny may have thought you were too young to understand the truth about Mom getting very ill and dying. I know it is confusing to get two different answers and not know which one to believe.

Maybe Aunt Jenny thought it would make you feel better to think your mom was away on a trip, but she didn't realize it would make you wonder about things. Your mom didn't go on a long trip, so she couldn't take you with her. She died of cancer. That is really what happened.

My mom died in the hospital. I am so sad. I am always looking for her. Is Mom a butterfly that goes by? Is she saying hello?
That's a good question. What do you think?

I think every time I see a butterfly, it is my mom saying hello. Is that OK?
Absolutely. Many adults and children believe their person that died is with them in some way. It can be a bird that flies by or even a passing breeze. No one really knows the answer. I think it's a very nice way to think of your mom. Would you like to wear a butterfly necklace to remind you of your mom? It might help you to feel your mom is with you.

If my mom is with me, is she watching over me all the time? That could be very embarrassing.
Watching over you can just mean feeling like your mom's love and caring is with you. It doesn't mean that she is looking at you all the time and seeing everything you say and do.

Joey (7): a case study

Joey was 7 when his big brother Alex was killed in a house fire. This sudden and traumatic death left Joey with a lot of questions: "Did Alex suffer? Did he know what was happening? What caused the fire?" – and the most pressing of all – "Do you think he is in heaven?" Joey wondered: "How could Alex get there by himself? Was God waiting? Suppose he needed medical help?"

I think Alex is in heaven. What do you think heaven is like?

What do you think about heaven? I bet we each have our own idea. Let's both draw a picture about it and share our ideas. We can draw the people and things and animals that are there and what they are doing.

OK. I think heaven is a place where everyone has a friend. There's a golden palace that only special people live in. Alex loved coffee so much. Do you think they have coffee shops in heaven?

They might. Nobody really knows exactly what heaven is like. It's really nice to imagine a person we love and care about is safe in a nice place like heaven. We can think of them having fun and doing all of the things they love.

My brother loved pizza and playing soccer. Do you think he is scoring goals in heaven?

He could be. I can imagine him running around the pitch and when he scores the winning goal, the angels hand him a big pizza. Can you remember a time you ever ate pizza and played soccer with Alex? Tell me about it.

Alex coached my soccer team and we always got pizza after the game. I think I'll wear his soccer shirt the next time I come. Is that OK?

That's perfect. I would love to see it. We can remember Alex together. Maybe he is wearing his soccer shirt in heaven.

I worry about my brother a lot. I have nightmares and can't sleep. I keep seeing his house on fire. If he was very injured and died, how did he get to heaven?

Joey, I know you have had a hard time sleeping and you wake up with nightmares. You see the house burning over and over in your mind. Children will often have bad dreams after someone they love is killed in a scary way. All of this is normal. Maybe you can tell me how you would like your dream to end. Can you think of a plan for Alex to get to heaven?

I think a huge fire truck with God as the chief lifted Alex into the clouds and took him to the Alex Rescue Medical Center in heaven. Doctors and nurses gave him bandages,

*medicine, and his favorite licorice and potato chips. Do
you think God is taking care of Alex?*
It sounds like you think heaven is a pretty special place.
You loved your brother so much and said he was such a
good person – it seems to me God would take wonderful
care of him.

*I think God is hugging Alex in heaven. He is happy and
laughing and has all the medicine he will ever need to feel
good.*
I bet that it can help you feel good to picture God and
Alex hugging. You can feel he is being taken care of. It's
nice to imagine Alex having the medicine he needs and
being healthy. In that way, you won't need to worry
about him suffering anymore.

*Sometimes I think Alex could get lonely in heaven. I hope
he has company. Do you think our dog Maxwell is with
him? That's our dog that died.*
I don't know. I hope so. Some people believe when you
go to heaven all of the people and animals you love are
there to greet you. Everyone looks and feels great and
has fun with each other. Others believe heaven is filled
with angels. Still others think heaven is a happy place in
your mind. The great thing about thinking about heaven
is that there is no right or wrong way. Heaven can be
whatever you imagine. What do you imagine?

Concluding thought

It is common to express hope in seeing a loved one again and finding a place of connection, whether it is the cemetery or Dad's office. Many children also locate their person in a place called heaven. It can be reassuring to envision Mom or Dad surrounded by angels, or friends and relatives doing something fun. They may be eating their favorite pizza, dancing to disco, or catching a giant fish. Sometimes it is helpful for children to draw a picture or tell a story about heaven. It helps children feel comforted and safe if they can hold a positive image of where their person is that died.

CHAPTER 5

My mom is dying.
What can I do?

It is important for children to feel included as an active member of the family if someone is very ill. Reminding them they can do lots of things to help during an illness allows for participation. Preparing them for the future if a loved one is terminally ill is also helpful. Children can then share feelings, ask questions, or engage in projects to work through a difficult time.

Sophie (8): a case study

Eight-year-old Sophie was told her mother had lung cancer. The disease had spread through her body and chemotherapy was no longer useful. Her mom explained to her that she was very, very ill and the doctors didn't think they could help her body get better. "The doctors aren't sure how long I will live. Nobody really knows. They say I could die. For now I am very ill."

Mom wrote a letter to Sophie for her to have on every birthday for many years to come, including memories, pictures, and important "Mom advice" for each year. She gave her the first one on her 9th birthday and reminded her another would be coming at 10.

Sophie created a video interview with Mom called, "My Favorite Person: Starring My MOM." She made a list of questions for Mom to answer and recorded everything. The questions ranged from Mom's childhood to memories of Sophie as a baby, and Mom's favorite colors and foods. They both had so much fun making it.

Nobody knew how long Mom would live, but Sophie knew she wanted to do everything she could to help her mom.

I'm so sad. I love my mom and she is dying. I want to help her. What can I do?

Sophie, it is very sad to think about your mom dying. Right now she is with you and there are things you can do to help her feel good. You could bake her favorite cookies, say a prayer with her, give her medicine, share a favorite story, or tell a funny joke. You can even sit quietly with her and hold her hand. That can be very comforting if she feels ill or tired. Is there anything special you would like to do?

I would like to give her something special of mine – my music box. Is that OK?

I think she would love it. Would you like to bring it here? We could go to the store and pick out special wrapping paper and bows. Then you could write a note to put inside. Maybe you could suggest for Mom to put it right by her bed. Then she could listen to the music and think of you.

Can Mom and I still do things together?

You can still do lots of things together. You love each other very much and it can feel good to tell each other that. You can eat dinner together, watch a movie, play a game, or sing songs. Every time you say goodbye to Mom, you can tell her how much you love her and give her a big hug. I think she would like that.

Rafi (6)

I heard my Mom say Grandpa is going to die. That makes me so sad. Is Grandpa really going to die?

Grandpa is very ill. He is old too. He had a heart attack a few weeks ago. The doctors and nurses are trying to help him get better, but he is still really, really ill. No one knows when someone will die, but the doctors *do* say Grandpa has a serious illness and could die soon. They don't know when.

How can I help Grandpa?

Grandpa still loves you very much and I know you love him. You can make a picture for him, say a prayer, or go visit him if you like.

I'll make a big heart with I LOVE YOU on the bottom.

Will I get to see Grandpa again? Where is he?
Yes, you can visit Grandpa if you would like. You can
bring him the big heart you made. He is in a place called
a hospice.

What is a hospice?
A hospice is a place where helpers work with Grandpa.
They are helpers for people who are very, very ill and are
not expected to get better. They make it easier for
Grandpa to feel the best that he can.

Some are doctors, nurses, and aides that care for him,
give him medicine, and help him feel comfortable and
not feel pain. Other hospice people are volunteers who
listen and talk with Grandpa to keep him company.
Some are social workers that answer questions for
Grandpa's family and friends and help them share stories
about Grandpa. There might even be a hospice dog to
pet.

Can I say goodbye?
Yes. That would be nice for you and Grandpa. Let me
prepare you for what you might see and hear. Grandpa
might not look the same. He may be thinner than the last
time you saw him. He may not talk, but he still knows
you are there. You can touch him, kiss him, and tell him
you love him. You can bring him a present too. You don't
have to stay long. You can leave whenever you're ready.

He may be weak and even cry. He may be getting
some medicine through his arm. You don't need to be

afraid. It is still Grandpa. You love him and he loves you. You can give him a hug too if you want to. Do you have any questions?

Can I bring flowers with my I LOVE YOU heart?
Of course you can. You can pick Grandpa's favorite color flowers. It feels good to bring something special.

I sat on Grandpa's bed and held his hand. He smiled at me and I smiled back. Then I squeezed his hand, said "I love you," and decided to leave. Was that OK?
That was perfect. You got to be with Grandpa and say goodbye and bring him special gifts. Remember, if you have any more questions about Grandpa, you can always ask me.

Jarrett (12): a case study

Jarrett loved Uncle Adam. They would hang out a lot together, going to the cinema, eating ice cream, or even skateboarding in the park. Then Uncle Adam got ill. Mom and Dad would whisper about his illness, but Jarrett caught a few words like AIDS and terminal. He didn't know what these words meant but he did know his parents were worried. Uncle Adam began losing weight, sleeping a lot, and not visiting much. He didn't seem the same.

What's wrong with Uncle Adam? Is it my fault?

Your parents have talked to me about Uncle Adam and shared their concern for him and why he is so sick. Uncle Adam has AIDS. AIDS is a serious disease but it is difficult for children to get it. When he seems so tired or angry or sad or irritated, it is part of having AIDS. It is not your fault. He is very ill, and might not live long.

What is AIDS?

AIDS stands for Acquired Immune Deficiency Syndrome. A rare virus called HIV weakens the healthy cells or immune system causing AIDS. The immune system keeps the body healthy. When it can't protect the body, infections and cancer can occur. People can live with AIDS for a long time. Medicine and treatment can help to kill germs, stop infections, and fight the virus. That's what's happening to Uncle Adam.

Why is it a secret?

Sometimes people are ashamed or embarrassed if they have AIDS and keep it a secret – thinking only a certain type of person or group can get AIDS. But this isn't true. Anyone can get AIDS. They can be rich or poor, African-American or white, old or young, Asian or Hispanic. There is a shame or stigma that may go along with having AIDS, but people don't get AIDS because of *who* they are; they get AIDS from contact with infected blood or having sex with someone that has AIDS.

Can I catch it?

You can't catch AIDS like you can catch a cold. You can't get AIDS from eating with someone, coughing or sneezing, swimming or playing sports, toilet seats or touching. AIDS is a sexually transmitted disease and you can get it through contact with someone else's infected blood.

What does terminal mean?

Terminal means the doctors think the person will die. No one knows when, but it means they are very, very ill. That's what the doctor said about your Uncle Adam. His illness is very serious and the time you can spend with him is precious.

Concluding thought

Too often children overhear whispers about an ill family member and imagine what is or what will be happening instead of knowing the facts. Adults may shut them out of difficult conversations because they don't seem to have the right words or fear it is inappropriate to include them. This only creates isolation for the child and wondering about what is really occurring in their family. Explaining what the illness is, how they can help, and words like hospice and terminal can prepare children for the future and give them permission to participate in the present.

CHAPTER 6

I am very ill.
Who can I talk to
about dying?

Children that are very ill have many special questions.
They need to be free to speak of issues about their own
life and death. Sometimes it is too difficult for others to
discuss their future and what will happen to them, or
simply to cope with their present condition. This can
create a feeling of isolation and alienation for an
extremely ill child. It is helpful to have a caring adult
who can be present and listen to any and all questions
and who can openly talk about future plans and options,
related issues such as how life may change, medical treatment, or even death concerns.

Emily (10): a case study

Emily is 10 years old. She has leukemia and has been
living with her illness for four years. Her oncologist, Dr.
Martin, has given Emily three rounds of chemotherapy.
This time he says it isn't working anymore.

Dr. Martin told Emily and her family she is seriously
ill and that he doesn't know if and when she will get

better. He doesn't know how long she will live. Her brother Max and sister Amy worry a lot too. It's hard for siblings. They want to help Emily and love her a lot. But sometimes they get jealous that people don't pay as much attention to them and only seem to ask about Emily and her illness.

Her mom and dad cry all the time. That's hard for Emily and she wishes she could make them happy. She also feels very alone because no one really wants to talk to her about dying and she wonders inside, "Won't anybody talk to me about dying?"

Well, living with cancer is hard. Living with it and knowing you might die is even harder. Will you talk about dying with me?

Emily, I know you have been sick for a long time. You and your family and Dr. Martin have tried so hard to help you get better. Now the doctors say you might not. Yes, I will talk to you about dying. I'm glad you feel you can trust me. What would you like to talk about?

Nobody wants to talk to me about dying – especially my mom and dad. They just cry. How can I make them feel happy?

I know it is hard to see your parents so sad. They love you so much. It is a great idea to think about what makes them happy. Can you think of something?

I know. They love to watch me dance. I want them to remember me as a beautiful ballerina, dancing in heaven. Do you think that would make them feel good?

Yes I do. Let's take a picture of you dancing in your best ballerina costume – the one you love the most. Then we can give it to Mom and Dad as a present. You can even pick out a beautiful picture frame to go with it.

My brother Max gets angry with me for being ill. He wants my presents. What should I do?

Sometimes brothers and sisters feel left out because adults talk so much about you and your illness. People might not ask them how they are and only ask about you. That makes them feel bad. Then you get lots of presents for being ill and they don't get any. I hope that helps you understand Max's anger.

Maybe you could help them feel special too. Let them know how much you appreciate their help and the things they do for you. Ask them how they are. There might even be a few presents you've received you can give to Max, or ask him which one he would like. It is good for you to realize that your illness affects the whole family, and your mom and dad and brother and sister have feelings about it.

Sometimes I wonder – when and where will I die?

No one knows when they will die, but they can plan where they would like to be. There are different places you can choose. You can stay in the hospital where doctors or nurses can take care of you and everyone you love can visit. You could also stay at home and pick a favorite room, or bed, or window to be near. Helpers and visitors can be with you there.

If I had a choice, I would like to die at home. But what will I do with all of my stuff?
You might think about which people are special to you and if you would like to give your things to them. We can make a list of the people and what you want to do with your things. Then we can give the list to your mom and dad. Let me know when you are ready and we can make a list.

My best friend Beth can have my dolls, and I think my brother Max would like my TV. My little sister Amy can have all of my stuffed animals – all except Tiger. Can I keep Tiger for me?
Of course you can. Why don't you make a list of all of your wishes?

I feel happy now. It feels good to talk about dying and make some plans. Now I feel I can go on living and not worry so much.

Concluding thought

Talking to critically ill children helps them cope with their present illness and creates a safe space to share concerns about dying. All too often family members find this too painful. Moms and dads and siblings need to be reassured that open dialogue can be beneficial for their loved one. If they are not able to speak about issues of illness and death, they can help find a caring adult that can hold this sacred space for discussion.

CHAPTER 7

I worry a lot.
Will I die too?
Will you die too?

Children are often worried after a sudden traumatic death. Immediately they may ask themselves the question, "How could this happen to me?" Their safe world is suddenly shattered, and the assumption that the adults around them can keep them protected is destroyed. Some children may begin to have nightmares, sleeplessness, and feel anxious or fearful, and they aren't really sure why. Others regress or panic when Mom or Dad are out of sight. So often they worry about their own health or that of a loved one.

Giving children *reality checks* about their own health can be reassuring. The pediatrician and school nurse are good resources and allies to ease their minds. The doctor can take their temperature, give medicine, and answer medical questions to help comfort girls and boys. Educators can also provide extra support for children. Interventions such as calling home, having a safe space to go to, picking a class buddy, and allowing extra teacher time create a tangible plan with student involvement.

When a death occurs children may worry about other family members dying too. Many girls and boys question, whether outwardly or unspoken, what would happen if their parents died. Asking the question out loud is an opportunity for parents to reassure their children that they will be taken care of, and invite them to be part of the decision-making process. In this way they may feel they have regained a sense of control after a traumatic death.

Peter (7): a case study

Peter was 7 years old. He died of a brain tumor soon after he fainted on the school playground. Peter had first complained to his teacher of a bad headache, then fell off the swings and became unconscious. His parents rushed him to the hospital, where the doctors discovered a brain tumor.

He died after an unsuccessful emergency operation. Peter's classmates and siblings had lots of questions about his death. They worried a lot about what could happen if someone gets ill. They worried their parents could die. They worried they could die too.

Scottie (7; Peter's friend in second grade)

Since Peter died I get lots of headaches. Will I die too?
You seem very healthy and that means you will probably live for a long time. Usually when we get ill we get better

all by ourselves or with the help of medicine and a doctor. If you get a headache it doesn't mean anything bad will happen to you. Let's ask your mom if you can visit your pediatrician, Dr. Jones. He can give you a physical exam and reassure you that you are OK. If you have any questions about your health or Peter's death, bring them along to the visit. Dr. Jones is a good person to help answer those questions.

I have one question. Can I catch what Peter had?
Peter had a rare illness that usually doesn't happen to children. It is called a brain tumor. You can't catch a brain tumor the way you can catch a cold. You can't get it from your parents the way you get blue or brown eyes from Mom and Dad. You can't get it just because you have a headache or fall off a swing.

Sometimes I think about Peter at school. I don't feel like eating and my tummy hurts. What should I do?
Scottie, the next time your tummy hurts you could visit the school nurse. She is a good helper right at your school that you can talk to. She might understand it is common for children to get stomachaches after someone dies. Sometimes their hurt or worry goes right to their tummy.

My worry does go right to my tummy. It hurts.
It is normal for worries to go to your stomach or another part of your body. Show me just where the worry is in

your tummy. Point to it for me. Take a deep breath right there, and then let it go. Put your hand on the sore spot and rub it a little. That might help to rub the worry away.

It is hard for me to pay attention in school. I daydream a lot and think I am going to cry when I think about Peter. Then I want to call home. What should I do?

I understand you have so many feelings in school, and you don't know when you might feel sad or worried. That makes it hard to concentrate on schoolwork. It might make you miss your mom a lot too.

Your mom and dad and I had a conference with Mrs. Novak. We made a plan to help you with all of these hard feelings in school. Here's what you can do. Call home once a day to touch base with Mom if you start to worry. You can pick the time. If you feel worried or upset in class you could pick a person to talk to, like the school nurse. Mrs. Novak will know where you are going if you suddenly feel sad and leave the room. You can choose a class buddy to make sure you get your homework assignments and help you with schoolwork. Mrs. Novak said she would give you special time to help with assignments.

Sarah (11; Peter's older sister)

I worry a lot that if Peter can die, my mom and dad can too. What would happen to me? Who would take care of me?

That's a good question. I think they will live a long time, but no one can promise when or where someone will die. We could ask them to have medical check-ups to reassure you they are OK.

Lots of children worry after a death about the health of other people in the family and what would happen if their parents died. Ask your parents when you are ready. I think they can reassure you someone will take care of you. They can tell you their plan or you can help them think about it. Maybe you even have an idea about who you would like to be with and let them know.

Julie (6; Peter's younger sister)

Since Peter died, I worry about going to sleep. If I sleep I have bad dreams. Will I die if I go to sleep?

No. Sleep is not the same thing as death.

But at Peter's funeral I heard my aunt say Peter is at rest. That makes me worry about even taking a nap.

You are safe to take a nap and go to sleep. Sometimes people use the words "rest" and "sleep" when they talk about death. It is not the same. Death is when the body stops working. Your body is working when you are resting and sleeping. Maybe your mom can leave a little light on in your room and you can sleep with your pal, Mr. Teddy.

But I still have so many nightmares. I wake up screaming and crying. What can I do to stop the worry?

There are some things you can do to stop the worries. Here are a few ideas. Make a worry box. Decorate it with pictures, stickers, and words that tell about your worries. Then put the worry inside. You can share it if you like, but you don't have to. List your top five worries. Share them with someone if you want to. Write a letter or draw a picture about your worries. Maybe tell Mom or Dad or a favorite teacher what you are worried about. Get a doctor's note after your parents have their medical exam. Keep a diary. It can even have a lock. Draw or write how you feel. It is a safe place for you to store worried feelings or share them with others. It is your choice.

Concluding thought

All of these children were impacted by Peter's death. Regardless of their age, it was natural for them to worry after a sudden trauma. Interventions that allow young people to release their worry can be very helpful in placing these worries outside of themselves. Actively involving children in exploring thoughts and feelings, expressing pent-up emotions, asking questions, and using reality checks can help to release these worries in safe and meaningful ways.

CHAPTER 8

Will I forget my dad? What if I forget him? How can I remember?

Memory work is a grief intervention to help children remember. So often adults and children fear they will forget their person. Mom's voice or Dad's face may fade into the past. Sharing stories, recalling special moments, creating rituals, and making memories into projects and books help to keep that special person alive in a healthy and safe way.

Margie (7): a case study

Margie was a 7-year-old whose dad died of pneumonia a few months before. Frightened by a nightmare, she ran into her mom's bedroom and woke her up sobbing: "Mom, I am so afraid I won't remember Dad. I can't hear his voice anymore and I'm scared. Will I forget it?" She burst into more tears. This is an all too common fear for children. How can we answer their questions?

I'm afraid I will forget my dad. What can I do to remember him?

It is scary to think you might forget your dad – the way he looked or sounded or felt. Sometimes we can do memory projects to help us remember. Do you have a favorite picture of you and Dad?

I know. I like the picture of Dad and me making a snowman.

That sounds like a good one. We can make a picture frame together for it and you can tell me all about that day. You can use lollipop sticks and glue and little stones. Then you can put it in a special place to help keep the memory.

Sometimes I can't remember his voice, or even what he looks like. That scares me. What if I forget my dad?

Your dad will always be in your heart. It's common for children to feel if they aren't thinking about their person all the time – then they have forgotten them and don't love them. It's OK. You don't need to think about Dad constantly to love and remember him.

You could ask all of your dad's friends and family to give you a story about your dad and a picture of him. You could put the stories and pictures of your dad in a special memory book. As you read each new story and see each new picture, it will help you not to forget Dad.

You can also listen to Dad's voice if you have a recording or see him on family videos. Do you have any?

*My sister saved Dad's voice on a mobile phone message.
My mom has a video of Dad and me. Can I share them
with you?*

That would be great. I would love to hear your dad's
voice and hear what he said. The video helps me see your
dad and you together. It is another good way to help you
remember and help me get to know your dad. You can
play them whenever you want so you don't forget.

Amber (12; Margie's older sister)

*I miss Dad so much. Mom's angry, Margie's sad, and
sometimes I can't even talk about it. What can our family
do to remember him together?*

It is important to remember Dad as a family. Sometimes
family projects let everyone share their grief and their
memories together. Grief support groups are helpful
where children and parents can come together and share
with other families. That way your family knows other
people going through grief too. You can share memories
as a family with others.

*Our family went to a support group together. We made a
big family banner about Dad and talked about it. Can I
show it to you?*

Your family banner tells a wonderful story. It lets people
know Dad loved purple, pizza, and football. You,
Margie, Jonathan, Mom, and Dad look like you're

having so much fun at the football game. It's a good memory. In fact, I think it's a great memory!

We shared the banner the last night of the group. I wore Dad's favorite purple hat and we brought a pizza for everyone to remember Dad. But how can we remember together at home?

One thing you can have at home is a memory table. Each person in your family can put something on it that reminds you of your dad. It can be a picture, a special note, or even Dad's ring. You can talk to each other about it if you like, or just leave it there for everyone to see.

I'll put my tape of Dad playing the guitar and a picture of Dad in his army uniform. He was in a rock-and-roll band.

Good idea for your memory table. You can even make a sign saying memory table and find a special place for it. Invite everyone in your family to join you.

Is there anything else our family can do together to remember Dad?

I have some suggestions. See which one you like. You could make a special garden in your backyard. Everyone can pick his or her favorite flowers to plant for Dad. A remembering ceremony might feel good on Dad's birthday. Everyone could have a balloon, write a special message on it, and send it off to your dad together. Your whole family could go to dinner at Dad's favorite restaurant and maybe even eat his favorite foods and share memories together.

It hurts to think about the holidays without Dad. It makes me sad. What can we do to remember Dad at Christmas?

Holidays can be hard after a person has died. They are times when the whole family should be together, and so it's natural to miss your dad. But it does help to do things that keep him there in spirit as you prepare for Christmas. It will help you remember Dad that day. There are lots of things you can do. Bake Dad's favorite gingerbread cookies for the holiday. Make a beautiful star for the top of your tree to remember Dad. Hang all the stockings on the fireplace, including one for Dad. You could even make it a family ritual on Christmas to have a beautiful candle to light just for Dad. You could all share memories together to remember your dad in happy ways.

Jonathan (10; Margie's older brother)

I like to draw and write. I think about Dad when I am alone and remember a lot. Can I make something about those memories?

I know you miss your dad very much. Since you like to write and draw, it might be fun to make a memory book about Dad. You can put in pictures of Dad, and important dates like his birthday and the day he died. You can make each page a memory about him. One page could explain how he died. Another could be your funniest memory. Still another might tell about your best memory or a time you can't forget. You could include your feelings, like sadness or worry, and what you do about them. You might even want to write Dad a letter or have a page that says goodbye. Sometimes there might be something you are sorry for. You could add that page too.

I have my dad's wallet. It means a lot to me. Can I make a special place to keep it?

Yes, you can make a place to keep special things that belonged to your dad. Let's call it a memory box. It can be a box that holds important items from your dad, like his wallet. You can decorate the outside with Dad's favorite color, and then find pictures, stickers, and words that remind you of Dad. Then put the wallet inside.

I'll keep the memory box next to my bed and put in Dad's old football cards too. It makes me feel close to him to have things he loved.

Concluding thought

Involving children in memory activities helps to keep their loved one alive in their hearts. Listening to a loved one's recorded voice or seeing photos and videos can help refresh a memory. Some of these activities are memory boxes, memory books, memory tables, memory rituals, and grief support groups. These can be useful ways to add meaning and comfort when remembering a person who died.

CHAPTER 9

Is it my fault my mom died? Did she suffer?

Developmentally, young children live in an egocentric world filled with the notion that they have caused and are responsible for everything. They have a great deal of magical thinking and often see themselves as having caused the death.

Only when this magical thinking about causing a death can be expressed will the burden begin to be released. Explaining the facts of a person's death is important, whether they are medical reasons or related to an accident or traumatic event. Adults can check to be sure children understand an explanation by asking them what they think they heard and repeat it. Sometimes children misinterpret the facts.

Children of all ages and adults can usually find a reason why their person died. They have so many "if only" and "what if"s. Sometimes blaming themselves helps them to feel like there is some control and reason over something that may appear so random. Older children have magical thinking too.

James (12): a case study

James was 12 when his mom was killed in a car crash. She had repeatedly asked him to go on the Internet and get directions to her meeting. He never got around to it. Frustrated and in a rush, Mom left the house saying, "I'll have to figure it out as I go, and I'm late."

That's the last thing she ever said to James. She hit another car at a stop sign and was immediately killed. The police said she was dialing a number on her mobile phone. James secretly thought she was dialing him for directions.

He blamed himself every day. He was continually plagued with asking himself the same question, "Who was Mom calling?"

Was she calling me when she died?

I know you worry that your mom was calling you when the accident happened. Possibly we can check her mobile phone and find out who she was calling so you know the facts. Maybe your dad knows.

Dad said she was calling him, not me. But I still should have gotten her the directions. Is it my fault my mom died?

No, it is not your fault. Your mom was responsible for getting the directions to her meeting, not you. You might be looking for a reason to blame yourself just to make sense of a terrible tragedy. You could be thinking if only you had gotten her the directions she wouldn't have made the call. It is common to play back in your mind all

of the things you should have done that day. We don't
know why your mom made the call, but we do know she
was driving and dialing her mobile phone at the same
time. That is a dangerous thing to do and may have
caused the accident.

Arthur (6)

*One time I was angry with my mom. I told her I wished
she were dead. Did that make it happen?*
Thoughts and feelings can't make a person die. That is
called magical thinking. You may begin to think your
words were so powerful they could make your mom die.
But they can't. Death is not like magic. Your mom hurt
herself very badly when she fell down. She had a heart
attack. That made her die – not your words.

*My mom picked me up the night she died. Then she had a
heart attack. Did that kill my mom?*
No, your mom lifting you up did not kill her. She had
heart disease that made her very ill. The doctors gave her
medicine, but she smoked cigarettes and was over-
weight. That made her heart disease worse. It wasn't
your fault Mom died. Her heart stopped working when
she fell down.

Suzie (7; dad killed in terrorist attack)

My dad had a cold the day of the attack. Couldn't I have saved him if I made him stay home that day? Why didn't I call him and warn him the terrorists were coming?

Often children feel they could have done something to prevent their person's death. It is very common. When you think back on that day, you can probably think of lots of ways you could have stopped what happened. But you didn't know it was going to happen at the time. What are some of your "if only" or "what if"s that go through your mind?

If only I had made my dad stay home, warned him on the mobile phone, or given him a big ladder to take to work to escape. I could have saved him. Is it my fault he died?

It is not your fault and you are in no way responsible. I know you wish you could have helped your dad with all of those good ideas but that would have been impossible. You didn't know what was going to happen. Some people did a very bad thing by surprising everyone in your dad's office with a bomb that hurt many people.

Michael (10; dad died in military combat)

I get so scared when I picture the way my dad died. I can't stop thinking about it. Do you think my dad suffered?

I can hear the anxiety in your voice when you talk about your dad's death. It must be so hard to keep thinking thoughts over and over again and picturing what happened. It is very common to have those thoughts and feelings after a sudden and traumatic death. It might help to draw what you pictured in your mind happened to Dad and tell me about it. That helps to remove it from your thoughts.

Here's my picture. The tank is exploding and Dad is on the ground. Look — he is all alone. Do you think he had help?

Your picture helps us to understand that one thing that is scaring you is thinking your dad was alone. Your dad was not alone. He was with two other soldiers who said they are willing to answer your questions. I can help arrange for you to speak with the two surviving soldiers and the medic on hand that day. Would you like to find out more about what happened when your dad died?

I do want to find out what happened that day. I want to know the facts.

I think that's a good idea. Before we talk with the soldiers and medic, let's make a list of what you would like to find out. I know you wondered if he was alone, did he suffer, and did he say anything before he died. Take some time and think about it. We can have the list of questions ready for the day of the meeting.

I'm glad I learned my dad wasn't alone and didn't suffer. It's nice to picture him surrounded with people who cared. It helps me not to worry about him so much.

Now you have a reassuring vision to hold next to your hard ones. Picturing Dad surrounded by people that cared about him and knowing he wasn't in pain helps let go of some of the worry. You don't have to guess about what happened now you know the facts.

I had a dream about my dad after our meeting. Dad was wearing his best uniform and gave me a hug. Do you think that means he is all right?

Maybe learning the details about Dad's death was helpful. I think it is comforting for you to think about that dream. Picturing Dad looking handsome in his best uniform giving you a big hug is special. Some children think their person may be visiting them in their dream. Others think it's a message that their person is OK, while still others just like to remember the good feelings. Nobody really knows the answer. But learning the details about your dad's death may have helped you relieve your worry about him suffering and open the way for a good dream!

Concluding thought

Listen not only with your ears, but also with a listening heart. Allow young people the opportunity to tell their entire story without interpretation, judgment, or preconceived notions. Try to uncover children's blame or worry by hearing their own questions, dreams, and visions. Answering honestly and providing accurate facts and details create an atmosphere of trust that permits kids to express and release guilt, fear, and magical thinking.

CHAPTER 10

How do other kids grieve? Sometimes I feel so alone

Children grieve differently from adults. Some children may be so sad, some may be angry, some may be frustrated, and some may appear not to be feeling anything at all. Adults often feel uncomfortable with the intensity of children's feelings and may unknowingly try to stop them expressing their feelings. Adults need to know what is *normal* for bereaved children in order to accept their unfamiliar thoughts, feelings, and behaviors. Children also need to know their grief reactions are common and OK. This helps children to diminish their anxiety and worry too.

One family member asked me about my work with grieving children. "What do you do to make the children stop crying?" I explained my goal was not to make children stop crying, but to create a safe haven for expression of all of their thoughts and feelings.

Often play is an important avenue for communication. What may appear to be a frivolous play activity may actually be a very profound way in which a child is working through their grief process. Role-playing, puppets, artwork, clay, and sand table work are a few of the many ways they can imagine, pretend, and engage in meaningful activities. This allows them to act out or project their grief feelings without having to verbalize them directly.

Kate (6)

My doggy Lucky died. I'm so sad. He got hit by a car and killed. Can I talk to Lucky?

I'm sorry Lucky got killed. I understand you are sad and miss him a lot. Sometimes it does help to feel like you can talk to Lucky. Here's a toy telephone. You can pretend to give him a call. At home you can sit and hold Lucky's picture in your hand while you talk to him. What would you say?

I love you, Lucky. I miss you a lot. I hope you're having fun and that God plays ball with you every day. Can I still help Lucky?

You can show me how you would like to help Lucky by pretending at the sand table or dollhouse or with puppets or toys. You can imagine you are with Lucky and show me some ways you can help him. Let's go to the sand table. Here's a dog like Lucky and a little girl like you. There's a car too, like the one that hit Lucky. You can make a street with your finger in the sand and show what happened.

I would have moved Lucky out of the way like this. I wish I could tell him I'm sorry. I wonder what he would say?

You pretend with the dog puppet and tell Lucky how sorry you are. Then Lucky the puppet can answer you back. You can imagine what Lucky would say and tell him how much you love him. You can even give him a hug and kiss and put a blanket around him.

I would say, "I love you, Lucky" and Lucky would lick my face. I like the sand table and puppets. They help me talk to Lucky.

My mom worries about me and says I act different. She thinks something is wrong with me. I'm tired a lot and nap with Lucky's toy on my bed where he slept with me. Is that OK?

That is not only OK, it is very normal. Children your age often like to have a special shirt or toy that belonged to their pet or person. You could even take Lucky's dog bed and make a pillow for yourself. You could make a special box to keep his collar in. It helps you feel close to Lucky.

And grieving is tiring. All of our energy goes into grieving and we don't even realize how tired it makes us. You have figured out a place where you can rest and also feel it's a spot where you can remember Lucky.

My dad thinks I should play with my friends the way I used to before Lucky died. But sometimes I'm sad and want to be alone. Do you understand?

I do. Lots of children feel they need time and space to grieve, and it can be hard to say and do the same things you did with your friends before Lucky died. Sometimes it's hard to have fun when you are feeling sad or even angry. Children can even feel guilty about having good times with friends – but you can still have fun and love Lucky too!

I made a list to give your parents about the common ways children grieve. That way they won't worry so much. I am going to share these ways with you too, so that you know you're not different because you have these thoughts and feelings. Many of the common signs of grieving children are the things you told me about. You like to be alone, you get tired, and you have found your bed as a place you can connect with Lucky. You like to sleep with his toy. It just makes you feel better. You like to pretend to talk to Lucky and want to know if you help him. This is all a part of the grief process.

Sometimes in school I think about Lucky so much I can't pay attention. Then my teacher gets angry with me and calls my mom. What can I tell her?

Your teacher needs to know what is common for grieving children too. Sometimes children can't pay attention or stay in their seats. They may call out of turn a lot, not talk at all, or forget their homework. That is because sometimes grief is overwhelming, and children don't know when they will get hit with a big wave of feelings. It may be at a time when they least expect it. It could be when the teacher reads a story about a dog and suddenly you are remembering Lucky.

Your parents could go to school and have a meeting with you and your teacher. I could go too. Your change in your schoolwork is an understandable part of all your feelings about Lucky's death. Your teacher is surprised at this change and doesn't understand it is related to your grief. You and I and your mom and dad can help explain that to her.

Here's what we can tell your teacher about grieving children so that she doesn't get scared or angry with you. Sometimes it is hard to do homework or sit still in class. It's difficult to concentrate and that might make you talk too much or not enough. Grieving children can withdraw from friends, or even become the class bully or class clown. There are a lot of behaviors that are common for children like you who have had a person or pet die. It is nice to know parents and teachers understand grieving children.

Concluding thought

Children grieve in their own unique way. It is essential that young people, parents, and educators become aware of what is common for the bereaved child in order to normalize new and challenging feelings and thoughts. Pretending, play-acting, and role-playing are creative outlets to express grief. Age-appropriate props and toys and techniques like drawing and writing are helpful for full expression. Creating a safe environment where children can share tears, frustration, silence, and imagination enhances a healthy grief process. While it can be uncomfortable to watch a child cry, it can be very healing at the right time and place.

CHAPTER 11

I'm scared too.
What can I do
to feel safe?

Children experiencing traumatic grief need to know their life will return to a calmer place. It takes patience and perseverance. Sometimes children are so shocked and frightened by a sudden or terrifying death of a loved one – they can hardly find words to talk about it. They are scared the same thing will happen to them or someone they love. They may seem frozen in time and unable to grieve.

As girls and boys begin to feel safer they can process their event. With reassurance and reminding that the difficult event is in the past, they are more capable of staying in the present and coping with their challenging thoughts and feelings. Reinforcing that they have survived a very difficult occurrence helps children feel stronger and more able to cope.

It is important to know the common signs of traumatic grief:

- hypervigilance or staying up all night
- nightmares and sleeplessness

- stomachaches and headaches
- regression – bedwetting, clinginess, fear of being left alone
- over and over repetitive thoughts
- reoccurring visualizations and re-enacting the traumatic event.

George (6): a case study

George witnessed the death of his older brother Tyrone. The whole family was eating at a fast-food restaurant when someone from Tyrone's school approached him and called him a name. They started yelling at each other and the manager told them to go outside.

Mom, Dad, and George could see them through the window. They began pushing each other and the other guy pulled out a knife and stabbed Tyrone. The rest of the family witnessed the murder, including George.

This sudden and traumatic death terrified George. He began showing signs of traumatic grief. George was hypervigilant as he incessantly looked out the window petrified something bad was going to happen. He had difficulty going to bed and when he did fall asleep, he would often wake up crying and sweating and calling for his mom. Every time he passed by that restaurant he would burst into tears: "Mommy, Mommy, I am so scared someone will die here like Tyrone did."

Why am I always so scared?

You witnessed a very scary thing when you saw your brother killed. It is hard to get it out of your mind and common for children to think about what happened a lot. But we are going to work together to help you not feel so scared.

It's so hard when a bad thing happens. You might feel life will never be the same again and don't know how to stop all of the sad, bad, and very big feelings you have.

You need to remember that the frightening thing that happened to Tyrone happened in the past, many weeks ago. It is not happening now. The person that killed Tyrone is in jail. He can't hurt anyone now. I will remind you when you get scared to check what is really happening now.

If my mom is late, is she at the restaurant where Tyrone got murdered?

George, I know you worry all the time about Mom and Dad. If Mom is a few minutes late to pick you up from school you often cry and begin to call her name. Your teacher told me you ran out of school to look for her. That's called "getting panicked something bad is happening." It's not. You are remembering the past and thinking it is happening now. The bad guy isn't at the restaurant and your mom could just be stuck in traffic.

But I think the bad guy is at the restaurant with Mom.
Why don't you get her mobile phone number and call her if she's late? Then Mom can tell you right then and there she is safe and not at the restaurant. I know she will be glad you called to check, so that she can reassure you she is all right.

Every time I realize Mom isn't at the restaurant, I feel better. But I still stay up at night and can't stop the bad thoughts. How could this have happened to me? What should I do?
You and your family are all in shock. You witnessed the killing together and it is hard for everyone in your family to sleep. Staying up and guarding the front door so that nothing bad happens is something children do when they have gone through a very hard experience.

Will these bad and sad feelings and thoughts ever stop coming?
The answer is yes. You have experienced a difficult thing and you are trying your best to get through it. You will. It might help you to know that the signs of trauma that you are showing are common. Staying up all night, having nightmares or stomachaches, thinking over and over thoughts, picturing the killing, and even bedwetting often happens.

I hit a boy on the playground because I knew he was going to hit me. I hit him before he could. Do other children feel like that after something bad happens?

Yes, George, it is all too common. It must be hard for you because you never hit children before Tyrone's death. The way you act has changed because you get afraid and think someone will hurt you or your family the way Tyrone got hurt. Remember, the boy on the playground isn't the bad guy. It is not happening now.

I get angry a lot. I feel like punching someone.

I don't blame you. I can't imagine how mad I would be if someone killed a person I love. But we can't hurt other people. There are safe ways to let go of your anger. You could punch a pillow, shout in the shower, take karate, or hit a punching bag. It might make you feel better.

Sometimes it helps to re-enact what happened to Tyrone and what you saw. It is something children might do. You could take toy figures, puppets, or play animals to show me what happened. I would like to hear about it. You could draw it on paper too.

It helps to get out my anger. I feel stronger now. I drew myself with big muscles and said, "This is me now. I am a lot stronger than I thought."

Jack (9): a case study

Jack's mom died in a car crash. She was driving too fast and hit a bus head-on. Mom had just dropped Jack off at school and was rushing to an appointment. She never saw the bus coming. Jack, like many kids impacted by traumatic grief, experienced over and over visualizations about the accident. He had repetitive thoughts too: "Why didn't I take the bus that day? Mom would still be alive."

Time went by and Dad began to go out with someone. Her name was Ann, the same as Jack's mom. It made him angry when Dad was with Ann. He missed Dad and he told a friend, "I'm afraid I will lose my dad too." This fear grew when Dad said he was taking Ann on a weekend camping trip in the mountains. Jack stormed out of the house, slammed the door, and screamed, "I won't let you!" When Jack calmed down, he went back in the house. Dad asked why he was so upset. "I'm afraid something will happen to you in the car, like Mom. Don't go." Dad suggested they brainstorm ways Dad could help Jack feel he would be safe. They made a plan.

I don't want my dad to go camping. I am afraid he will get killed too. What can we do to help me feel he will be safe?
Jack, your mom's death was so sudden it can be hard to think the world is safe. If your mom can get killed in a car crash, it makes you worry other people you love can get killed that way too. That is scary.

You asked a good question and I know we can think of some ideas to help you feel safe. Because you are very concerned about car safety, you could ask Dad to have the brakes checked, and the tires, and promise to wear seat belts and use air bags. Do you think that will help?

I like that idea. I want them to take the van. It is the safest. But will they call me?

We can ask Dad to call, and you and Dad can choose a good time. You can be sure to have Dad's mobile phone number in case you need to reach him, and Aunt Jane's or Grandma's number in case you want to talk to someone close by. We can make a schedule of Dad's trip and you can mark off the days as they go by. You could even keep Dad's picture by your bed and remind yourself he is OK. Let's make a list of all the ideas and give them to Dad. If he agrees, you both can sign it.

Dad and Jack's list

1. Dad drives a car with air bags.

2. Dad and Ann promise to wear their seat belts.

3. Dad will call at 7 p.m. every day.

4. Jack can have Dad's mobile phone number in case he needs to call.

5. Dad gives Jack Grandma's phone number and Aunt Jane's too.

6. Dad gives Jack a schedule of the trip.

7. Dad brings Jack a surprise.

Dad said OK to everything and was happy to do it. We even added that Dad would bring me back a surprise. I feel better now. But I still get scared something bad will happen again.

Jack, when your mom died suddenly in a car crash you experienced a trauma. A trauma is a sudden and very difficult thing that happens which is shocking. You, like so many children who go through trauma, feel bad things will never stop happening and your world will never be the same. But in time that feeling will get less.

I want to help you feel as safe and comfortable as I can. I want to help you feel you still have choices in life and can do things to help yourself feel stronger and less afraid. Why don't you try and use visualizations? This is when you imagine a happy place, using all of your five senses of touch, taste, smell, sight, and hearing. Decide if you would like to keep your eyes open or closed. You could visualize a beach, feeling the sand on your feet and the warm sun overhead – or – a peaceful forest with birds chirping and a rainbow bridge to walk across with Mom.

Or you could try drawing peaceful pictures. Draw something that makes you feel calm. It could be sky with birds or a lake with blue water. You can keep the picture in your room and look at it when you feel afraid.

I think I will draw green trees with beautiful birds of every color flying in the breeze or perched on a branch. I think I will feel happy when I look at that picture. What else can I do?

One thing you can do to feel safe is to create an emergency plan. You can decide where everyone would meet in case of a traumatic event, and make a list of important phone numbers to have. You could even design an emergency kit for home, and think about what would be helpful to put in there.

You could also try making a safe box. Cover a box with your favorite color and decorate it with stickers, words, and pictures. Then you can put in favorite pictures of Mom, a comforting toy, a special card from Mom, or a list of your top five things you loved about her. You can put anything meaningful inside. It could be the prayer you and Mom would say at night or her lucky penny. The safe box might fit in your backpack or under your bed.

Comfort food is nice too. Sometimes a fun snack or a great meal can make you feel cozy inside. I call that comfort food. Comfort food can be vegetable soup, mashed potatoes and meatloaf, with apple pie for dessert. We can make a menu for a comfort food dinner and ask your aunt if she would make it.

I want roast beef, baked potatoes, and cherry pie. It makes everything seem normal again to think about having that dinner with everyone. Mom used to make that for all of us and it was delicious!

Concluding thought

Children experiencing traumatic grief often feel frightened. This fear can override grief and stop their grief process. Providing safety for children is essential. Sometimes it takes time and distance. We can give them activities that help create the feelings of a protected atmosphere – like safe boxes, emergency plans, peaceful pictures, visualizations, and comfort food. As children realize their overwhelming thoughts and fears won't last forever, they can begin to explore their grief process. This process can be unpredictable and sometimes messy – as there is no correct order or timing for a child's grief.

CHAPTER 12

How can I remember with my friends and family? Can I go to the funeral too?

Many adults are very uncomfortable about including children in death-related issues and activities, and therefore leave them out. Some adults may think they don't have the perfect way to explain funerals and memorials. Others feel powerless when children are sad or cry, and sometimes adults inhibit tears and try to stop the grief process, usually without realizing that's what they are doing.

Children become recognized mourners when adults create ways for them to ask questions and share thoughts and feelings about a loved one who has died. *Preparing and inviting*, but never forcing, children to participate in funerals and memorials creates an inclusive environment. This nurturing space supports their emotional and spiritual growth as human beings by being actively involved in commemorating.

Jason (6): a case study

Jason was 6 years old when his best friend, Wyatt, died of a rare form of cancer. Every night Jason asked his mom the same question: "What is Wyatt doing in Heaven?" Mom responded in many ways: "Maybe Wyatt is with God. Maybe he is having fun. I'm not really sure." It became a bedtime ritual to think about Wyatt being in heaven and comforting to wonder about good and happy things.

One morning Jason excitedly ran to his mother's bedroom and exclaimed, "I know what Wyatt is doing. He loved fishing so much. I think he is catching the *biggest fish ever!*"

Jason, his classmates, and the entire school were in deep mourning. His teacher, Mrs. Jones, and the principal, Mr. Arnold, realized the children needed to be part of Wyatt's commemoration and memorial service. They permitted Jason and all of the students to become identified mourners by allowing them to ask questions, participate in activities, share thoughts and feelings, and be invited and prepared for Wyatt's memorial service.

What should we do with Wyatt's desk?

You and your friends can decide what to do with Wyatt's desk and the things inside. You could leave it in your classroom as a place children could go to and be with Wyatt. Students could leave special notes, drawings, and photos there to remember Wyatt. You could also decide to take the desk out.

What can we do with the stuff inside?
You have many choices about deciding what to do with "the stuff" inside Wyatt's desk. You could leave it there just the way it is or invite Wyatt's parents to take his things. You could also have all the kids that wanted to take something to keep that would feel like a part of Wyatt.

I miss Wyatt a lot at school. So do my friends. What can we do to remember him at school?
It is hard when you miss your friend at school. Doing something to remember him with friends helps you to feel better. Your class can have a meeting to brainstorm ideas about creating a memory project at school. Here are a few suggestions. Children can plant a flower, blow bubbles, bake a cake to bring to Wyatt's family, make a memory mural, or put together a class quilt to give to Wyatt's parents.

We had a class meeting and decided to bake his favorite peanut butter cookies, make a class mural, and create a class quilt. Can you help us with that?
The cookies sound like fun to make. You could eat some in school, bring some home for your family, and make a batch for Wyatt's family. The mural is a good group project. Everyone can draw or write a memory or message to Wyatt. You can leave it in your classroom all year and add a note whenever you feel like it. At the end of the year you could give it to Wyatt's parents as a

special gift for them. The class quilt could be made in squares, with the handprint of each child in Wyatt's class. It could be presented to Wyatt's parents at his upcoming memorial service.

What is a memorial service? Can I come?

A memorial service is a time when family and friends come together to remember the person that died. It might be at a church or synagogue, at someone's home, or even at school. Wyatt's memorial service is going to be at the community center building down the street from school. His family is going to have the service in a few weeks. Everyone that loved Wyatt can come together to remember him. You are invited to come, as are all the other classmates.

Let me prepare you for what it will be like. Parents, children, friends, relatives, and teachers can come. Pictures and memories of Wyatt will be all around the room. There will be bubbles for children to blow to remember Wyatt and an art table to draw or write a memory. Some people may be sad and cry, others might not do anything at all. That is OK. Wyatt's teacher, Mrs. Jones, is going to sing Wyatt's favorite song, "If you're happy and you know it" with the children. Wyatt's mom and dad will give all of the children a memory bag filled with things they feel Wyatt would want his friends to have. Your class can present them with the beautiful quilt you made. Would you like to go?

Can we share memories at the service?
Yes, children and grown-ups can share memories if they like. You can share a memory or favorite picture but you don't have to.

I want to share my picture of Wyatt and me on the junior soccer team. Can I do that?
Of course you can. I think it would be wonderful to share the soccer picture. You might tell the story you told me about Wyatt scoring his famous goal that won the game. You could even make extra copies of the picture for everyone to take home.

Jeremy (9)

My grandfather died. Where do they put his body?
Grandpa's body will be at the funeral – inside a casket or special box. Some caskets are made of wood and others of metal. They have handles so the casket can be carried. Sometimes the casket is open and there is a viewing where people can look at the body. Other families choose to keep the casket closed.

You don't need to be afraid of seeing the dead body. You don't have to look if you don't want to. The person cannot see or hear you. You can touch the body if you want, but you don't have to. It may feel cool to you. You can put a special picture, toy, or other object inside the casket. It might feel nice to do that.

What is a funeral? Can I go?

A funeral is a special time to say goodbye to Grandpa.
Friends and family will come together to honor his life.
The casket is at the front of the room. There may be
plants and flowers, and even music.

A priest, rabbi, or minister usually talks about the
person that died. Grandpa's friend, Father O'Malley, will
do that. Other people may tell stories or share memories
about Grandpa. Others may sit quietly or even cry. Any
way you feel is OK. Your mom and dad told me they have
invited you to come to the funeral. If you think of any
questions about it, please ask.

*My grandma was talking about going to the cemetery to
put Grandpa's body in a grave. What is a cemetery? Can
children go?*

Yes, children can go to the cemetery. It is a place where
Grandpa will be buried in the ground. After the funeral
the casket is carried to a hearse or funeral car. Relatives
and close friends may ride in a big car called a limousine
while others follow in their cars in a big line called a
funeral procession.

The cemetery is a pretty place with trees and plants.
Lots of people's bodies are buried there. Grandpa will be
buried in the ground. People gather together while this
is happening and sometimes they say a prayer or other
words to say goodbye to him.

Jeremy, your mom and dad are happy for you to come
to the cemetery. Would you like to think about it for a

while? It is a place we can visit on Grandpa's birthday or holidays, if we choose.

My friend Rick says his grandpa wanted to be cremated instead of buried. What does cremation mean?
Cremation is placing someone's body in a machine called a crematory. A crematory is a very hot chamber with heat so hot that a body turns to ashes. Then the ashes are put in a container called an urn or even a wooden box. Sometimes families choose to keep the ashes in the urn or box, while other people scatter them in the ocean, spread them in a forest, or bury them in the garden.

What happens to the body?
Let's remember that the body of Rick's grandfather stopped working completely when he died. He couldn't eat or read or feel anything. Nothing hurt him anymore. It's like his body is a costume with no person inside. The costume experiences nothing and has no life energy or thoughts or feelings. Some people believe that life energy or spirit goes to God or heaven or stays in the breeze we feel. Others say they just don't know.

Is it better to be cremated or buried?
They are both choices people can make before they die. One is no better or worse than the other. Whether someone is buried in the ground or cremated, you can still say a prayer for them with your family or friends, tell

a story about them, or plant a special tree to remember them by.

I am glad you are asking questions about the funeral, burial, and memorial service. By being allowed to participate and being prepared to attend commemorations, you become an important member of a community grief team. You can see you belong with your friends and relatives as they come together to honor your grandfather. Sharing memories and rituals with others helps to say goodbye to Grandpa.

Concluding thought

Young people can actively commemorate in their grief process by being prepared, invited, and being given choices about attending a memorial service or funeral. Children can become an active part of a ceremony just by sitting with family members, blowing bubbles, sharing, listening, and drawing pictures for their loved one or friend. Participating in age-appropriate ways gives meaning to their grief process as they come together with others in the community to say goodbye to a loved one. Saying goodbye to a loved one conveys a sense of dignity and respect for the person that died, and involving children in the commemorative process conveys a sense of dignity and respect for them as well. It gives a strong message about the value of all life.

A final note

We can't protect children from life's tragedies, but we can ease their journey by responding openly to their questions.

Encouraging a child's questions about death is essential in developing an understanding of the child's grief process. Too often children are given the message not to speak of their loved one, not to express their feelings, and not to ask questions. Adults often prescribe quick fixes and remedies based on the myths and clichés that they were raised with. Many girls and boys are told to be strong, be brave, and be the man or woman of the house. Or they are told that boys don't cry and children are too young to understand.

Yet, few children in this new millennium are exempt from issues concerning death. Issues ranging from the death of a parent to the loss of a pet can disrupt and confuse a child's emotional and physical stability. Many children experience fear, isolation, and loneliness after a death. Their new world seems to have no future, no protection, and no role models.

Girls and boys commonly and naturally assume that the world of grown-ups will care for them, support them, and nurture them. When Grandma has a sudden, fatal heart attack, Mom is killed in a car crash, Dad dies of suicide, sister Mary overdoses on drugs, or brother Thomas is fatally wounded in the military, a child's world *is* shattered. Often their *only* question is, "How could this have happened to me?"

Parents, teachers, and other caring adults need to be prepared to respond to children's questions. Grieving children in today's world are becoming a larger and larger growing segment of our youth and their grief issues arise at younger and younger ages. In the past, parents may have been advised to exclude children from memorializing and not to speak of death or their person that died.

In today's world it is not only important to include children – it is mandatory. Repression around difficult feelings involving death can lead to low self-esteem and depression, or projected anger and destructive behavior. We must assist our children in communicating on this delicate topic of death. Open and comfortable sharing with young people allows free expression of the natural flow of their grief process and ensures a safe haven of respect and honesty.

A checklist for children

- Know the facts about your person's death.
- Create a list of important questions to be answered.
- Be prepared for the funeral. Decide if you want to go.
- Participate in commemorating your person.
- Find three people you can really talk to about your thoughts and feelings.
- Use a memory book. Include pictures of your person and important memories.
- Design a memory box. Decorate it with pictures or words that tell about your person. Put something special of theirs inside.
- Invent a memory project. You can put together a pillow from Dad's shirt or think of an original poem or song.
- Make a memory mural or video to share memories of you and your person.
- Ask questions.
- Keep a safe box in your room with pictures and toys that make you feel good.
- Have a memory table. This is a place where everyone can leave something special that reminds

them of their person who died to share with others.

- Have a picture of you and your person, or draw one of a favorite memory.
- Have a locked diary. Your feelings and thoughts can be safely stored.
- Write down your everyday ideas in a journal.
- List your top five worries. Then tell someone about them.
- Know what is normal for grieving children.
- Read stories that help you with your grief.
- Perform a ritual for your person. You can light a candle, plant a flower, blow bubbles, say a prayer, or send off a balloon.
- Tell your teachers you are grieving. Find a class buddy to help you during your time of grief.
- Talk about your person if you want. That is OK.
- Go to a place where you feel you can be with your person.
- Be with good friends. Continue to play and have fun.
- Remember death is a natural part of life. It's OK to talk about it and that may help you feel better.

For caring adults

We must meet the needs of our grieving youth in today's world. With constant media bombardment and instantaneous communication, there are no secrets. Children today are savvy about issues of death and their questions are quite sophisticated. They deserve honest and respectful responses to their inquiries. Our goal is to prepare and create an open climate by honoring questions, knowing the common signs, and providing language for dialogue. This climate provides an important opportunity to facilitate a child's grief process and enhance his or her resilience.

Common signs of grieving children
Grieving children can...
- become the class clown or bully
- seem withdrawn and unsociable
- have bedwetting or nightmares
- appear unable to concentrate
- act impulsively
- not complete schoolwork
- show difficulty listening and being focused
- appear overly talkative, disorganized, and unable to follow directions
- demonstrate recklessness

- have poor concentration around external stimuli
- complain of stomachaches or headaches.

They may…

- talk to their loved one in the present
- imitate gestures of the person that died
- idolize the person who died
- create their unique spiritual beliefs
- worry excessively about their health and the health of others
- worry about death
- show regressive behaviors (clingy, babyish, etc.).

What can we do?

Be truthful. Children have a conscious or unconscious knowing if they are not told the truth. Then they suffer another loss of trust of the adults around them.

Keep explanations simple. More is not always better. Children are often content with a simple answer, knowing they can come back if they have more questions.

Share the facts. In simple and concrete language, share the facts with children about what happened to their person in age-appropriate ways.

Remind children it was not their fault. Too often children are filled with magical thinking and can too easily find a reason why they caused their person to die.

Define death. Death is when the body stops working. Usually people die when they are very, very old, or very, very sick, or their bodies are so injured that the doctors or nurses can't make their bodies work anymore.

Allow children to be recognized mourners. Invite and prepare children to be part of the family grief process. They can read a poem at the memorial, place a picture in Grandfather's coffin, or plant a flower for their dog Scruffy.

Remember children grieve differently. Boys and girls grieve differently from adults. What may appear to be a frivolous play activity may actually be a very profound way youngsters are processing their grief. Mary came to grief therapy and explained she really missed her mom. She took the toy telephone and pretended to give her a call. "Hi Mom. How are you? Are you OK? I really miss you. Let me tell you about my day."

Treat every child and their grief as unique. Children grieve as differently as they are individuals. Mary might cry and share her feelings, Lionel has nightmares, and Alex keeps a journal. Everyone is different and that is OK.

Include children in family illness. An ill family member that may be terminally ill is a challenge for all family members. By including children it allows them to understand what is going on, participate in helping, and be prepared for what may happen in the future.

Honor a child's belief system. Children begin to formulate their own spiritual belief system at a young age. Feeling their person is with them, or with God, can be important in their healing process. Respecting their experience is essential.

Prepare children for funerals and memorials. Children should be prepared and invited to these events, but never forced. They should be invited to ask questions about the service, and see how the community comes together to honor a life and say goodbye.

Useful websites
and children's resources

Websites

International organizations

www.adec.org

The Association for Death Education and Counseling is an organization dedicated to promoting excellence and recognizing diversity in death education, care of the dying, grief counseling, and research.

United States

www.childrensgrief.net

Helping Children Deal with Grief by Linda Goldman is a website that provides information, resources, and articles to help adults work with grieving and traumatized children.

www.griefnet.org

Griefnet is an internet community dealing with grief and death in families.

www.barrharris.org

Barr-Harris Children's Grief Center is an organization that provides resources, books, and assistance for children who have experienced the death of a sibling or parent.

www.speakforthem.org

> SPEAK – Suicide Prevention Education Awareness for Kids is an organization that works to prevent youth suicide and to dispel the social stigma surrounding suicide.

United Kingdom

www.winstonswish.org.uk

> Winston's Wish is an organization that helps grieving children after the death of a parent or sibling.

www.jeremiahsjourney.org.uk

> Jeremiah's Journey is a UK-based charity that provides support and information for bereaved children and their families.

www.childhoodbereavementnetwork.org.uk

> The Childhood Bereavement network provides information, guidance, and support for bereaved children and young people.

www.childbereavement.org.uk

> Child Bereavement Charity is a charity providing services to bereaved children. They also provide support, information, and training to all those affected when a child dies.

www.crusebereavementcare.org.uk

> Cruse Bereavement Care provides services for the well-being of bereaved people.

Canada

www.patchforkids.ca

> PATCH – Parents And Their Children Healing is an interactive grief support program for young children. London, Ontario.

Australia

www.anglicare-sa.org.au/services/starbear.html

> Anglicare Loss and Grief Star Bear Program for children ages 5–16 who are grieving. Southern Australia.

www.mcsp.org.au/arbor

ARBOR – Active Response Bereavement Outreach for families bereaved by suicide. Western Australia.

www.earlychildhoodaustralia.org.au

Early Childhood Australia is an organization that provides information and links for grieving children. Australia-wide organization.

www.nalag.org.au

National Association for Loss and Grief (NALAG) is an organization aimed at increasing community awareness and response to bereavement issues. New South Wales.

www.bereavementcare.com.au

National Centre for Childhood Grief (A Friend's Place) is an organization which provides services for children's bereavement. New South Wales.

Resources for children

Bart Speaks Out: Breaking the Silence on Suicide

by Linda Goldman (1996, Los Angeles, CA: WPS Publishers). This is a useful interactive storybook for young children that provides words to use for the young child to discuss the sensitive topic of suicide (ages 5–10).

Children Also Grieve: Talking to Children about Death and Healing

by Linda Goldman (2005, London: Jessica Kingsley Publishers). This is a beautiful illustrated interactive storybook and memory book for children who have experienced the death of a loved one (ages 5–11).

Grandad's Ashes

by Walter Smith (2007, London: Jessica Kingsley Publishers). This beautifully illustrated storybook is an ideal resource for parents or counselors to read with a child as a way of broaching issues surrounding loss or bereavement (ages 4–8).